The Louisiana Purchase

by Michael Burgan

Content Adviser: Harry Rubenstein,
Curator of Political History Collections, National Museum of American History,
Smithsonian Institution

Social Studies Adviser: Professor Sherry L. Field,
Department of Curriculum and Instruction, College of Education,
The University of Texas at Austin

Reading Adviser: Dr. Linda D. Labbo,
Department of Reading Education, College of Education,
The University of Georgia

COMPASS POINT BOOKS

Minneapolis, Minnesota

Compass Point Books
3722 West 50th Street, #115
Minneapolis, MN 55410

Visit Compass Point Books on the Internet at *www.compasspointbooks.com* or e-mail your request
to *custserv@compasspointbooks.com*

Photographs ©: North Wind Picture Archives, cover, 4, 5, 14, 15, 19, 21, 24, 28; Hulton
Getty/Archive Photos, 8, 10, 12, 13, 20, 23, 26, 27, 33, 34, 37, 39, 41; Stock Montage, 9, 16, 17,
18, 35; Bettmann/Corbis, 31.

Editors: E. Russell Primm, Emily J. Dolbear, and Deborah Cannarella
Photo Researchers: Svetlana Zhurkina and Jo Miller
Photo Selector: Linda S. Koutris
Designer: Bradfordesign, Inc.

Library of Congress Cataloging-in-Publication Data

Burgan, Michael.
   The Louisiana Purchase / by Michael Burgan.
     p. cm. — (We the people)
   Includes bibliographical references and index.
   Summary: Looks at the political and economic history of the region between the Mississippi
River and the Rocky Mountains which, when purchased by Jefferson in 1803, doubled the size of
the United States and led the way to further expansion.
   ISBN 0-7565-0210-1 (hardcover)
   1. Louisiana Purchase—Juvenile literature. 2. United States—Territorial expansion—Juvenile
literature. [1. Louisiana Purchase. 2. United States—Territorial expansion.] I. Title. II. We the
people (Compass Point Books)
   E333 .B87 2002
   973.4'6—dc21   2001004740

TABLE OF CONTENTS

A VAST FRONTIER

The heartland of the United States lies between the
rushing waters of the Mississippi River and the snowy
peaks of the Rocky Mountains. For thousands of years,
only the Native Americans who lived there knew about

The high plains of what is now Montana

4

this vast area of plains, fields, and forests.

The Spanish were the first Europeans to explore the region in the mid-sixteenth century. In 1682, France claimed most of this land and the land east of the Mississippi, too. They called this large area Louisiana. Famous explorers—such as René-Robert Cavelier, Sieur de la Salle, Jacques Marquette, and Louis Jolliet—sailed the Mississippi

René-Robert Cavelier, Sieur de la Salle

River and the smaller rivers that flow into it. French trappers roamed the woods and traded with the Indians. In 1718, the French founded the city of New Orleans at the mouth of the Mississippi River.

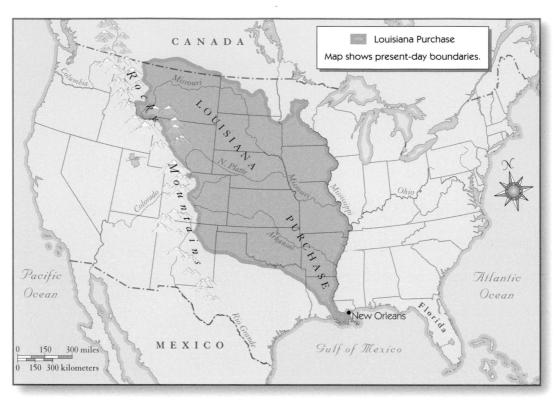

A map of the United States showing the Louisiana Purchase

Soon, both Spain and Great Britain also wanted
Louisiana. These countries claimed lands on the region's
border. In the French and Indian War, Britain fought
France for control of parts of North America. The British
won Canada and the part of Louisiana east of the
Mississippi River.

After the Revolutionary War, American pioneers

6

wanted to settle Louisiana, too. The country almost went to war to gain Louisiana and the rights to the Mississippi River. Finally, without firing a shot, the United States owned Louisiana. President Thomas Jefferson bought the land from France in 1803. This event, called the Louisiana **Purchase**, doubled the size of America. In time, it helped the country grow all the way to the Pacific Ocean.

SPANISH LOUISIANA

The French and Indian War was difficult for France. Louis XV, the king of France, asked his cousin, Charles III, the king of Spain, for help. When Britain won the war in 1763, it took some of the lands that belonged to Spain.

King Louis XV of France

To make up for Spain's losses, Louis XV offered western Louisiana to his cousin. King Louis did not want the region because it did not produce much wealth. He believed that New Orleans—a center for shipping on the Mississippi River—was the only valuable part of Louisiana. The rest of the vast region was rugged and natural, the homeland of many

The port of New Orleans in the early 1700s

Native American tribes, such as the Sioux. It had been difficult and expensive for the French to settle there. King Louis was glad to give the region to Spain.

The land was valuable to King Charles, however. Spain owned land farther west and south of Louisiana. This **territory** was called New Spain. It included lands that are now Mexico and the southwestern United States. By owning western Louisiana, Spain could protect New Spain

9

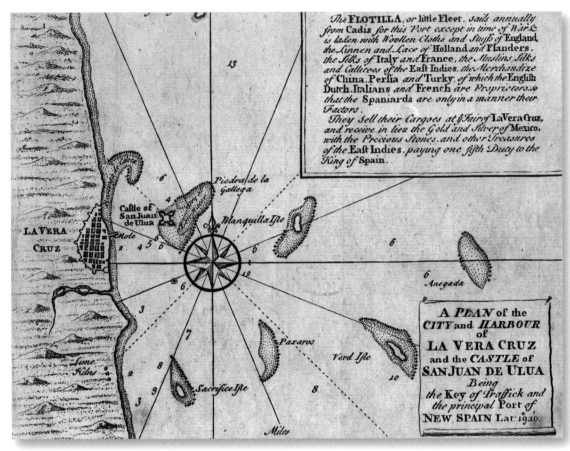

La Veracruz, on the Gulf of Mexico, was the principal port of New Spain as seen in this map from about 1750.

from future attacks by the British. Spain accepted the "gift" of western Louisiana—which became known as Spanish Louisiana.

In 1763, the British took control of eastern Louisiana, the land between the thirteen American colonies and the Mississippi River. Spain did not have an easy time with its new British neighbors. Great Britain now owned forts near the Mississippi River. It also began to control trade in Spanish Louisiana. Additionally, the British encouraged Native Americans to raid the Spanish settlements. Spain did not have enough military strength in Louisiana to fight the attacks.

FIGHTING FOR THE RIVER

During the Revolutionary War, the colonists fought for independence from Great Britain. France and Spain hoped the American **rebels** would win the war. Great Britain was their **rival**, too, and they wanted that country to lose some of its power. In secret, the French and Spanish gave

American colonists preparing for battle against the British

Delegates signing the Treaty of Paris to end the Revolutionary War

weapons to the Americans. The Spanish governor also bought Americans supplies in New Orleans.

By 1779, the French and Spanish began helping the Americans fight the British. With their help, the American colonists won their independence. In 1783, the **Treaty** of Paris was signed, and the war ended.

Spain would not let U.S. ships enter the mouth of the Mississippi River.

The United States had won eastern Louisiana. Spain was glad to have the British out of the region, but new problems were about to begin. The Treaty of Paris gave the United States the right to travel freely on the Mississippi River—now the country's western border. Spain, however, still controlled the river and did not want Americans to use it. In 1784, Spain closed the mouth of the river to U.S. ships.

Americans in the region were angry. Many settlers had begun to travel west even before the Revolutionary War ended. The farmers and merchants there needed the Mississippi River to ship their goods.

The U.S. government could not agree on how to solve the problem of the river. People in the eastern states did not care about the Mississippi River. The Atlantic Ocean was their trade route. Lawmakers in the western

American merchants shipped goods down the Mississippi River on flatboats.

and southern states, however, knew that the river was important to their success and growth.

In 1785, John Jay tried to make an agreement with Spain. He was in charge of the U.S. Department of Foreign Affairs. Jay said that the United States should promise not to use the river for twenty-five to thirty years. The country would, however, keep the right to use the river in the future.

John Jay was the U.S. secretary of foreign affairs from 1784 to 1789

Americans argued about Jay's plan. James Madison, an important leader from Virginia, was against it. He said, "The use of the Mississippi is given by nature to our western country, and no power on earth can take it from them." Jay warned the U.S. Congress that it would have to settle the problem with a treaty or go to war with Spain. Congress was not ready for war, though. It took ten years to write a treaty that both parties would sign. In the meantime, Spain let American ships use the Mississippi River—for a fee.

James Madison opposed John Jay's plan.

Thomas Jefferson was an important statesman from Virginia. He knew that the settlers were angry about the Mississippi River problem. Some of them had even talked about breaking away from the United States to become part of Spanish Louisiana or

Thomas Jefferson wanted to add western lands to the United States.

to form their own country. Jefferson agreed that the
Mississippi River was important for trade. He also wanted
the United States to explore the lands west of the river
and, one day, to make them part of America.

18

In 1783, Jefferson wrote a letter to George Rogers Clark, an old friend and a hero of the Revolutionary War. He asked Clark to lead an **expedition** to explore "the country from the Mississippi to California." Jefferson wanted to beat the British to those unknown lands. Clark never made the trip, but Jefferson never lost his interest in the West.

George Rogers Clark was a famous brigadier general during the American Revolution.

TWO TREATIES

In 1789, there was a revolution in France. The new government began to look for ways to get Louisiana back from Spain. The country was also still competing with Great Britain, and, in 1793, France declared war on its longtime enemy.

President George Washington did not want the United States to become involved in this or any other war in Europe. He said the United States would remain neutral,

George Washington

which meant that it would not support either side in the war. Some American people felt loyal to the French, however. They remembered that France had helped them during the Revolutionary War. These Americans supported France's fight against the British.

Edmond Charles Genet

As the new war began, the French government sent Edmond Charles Genet to America. "Citizen Genet," as he was called, looked for Americans to help France fight against Britain. He illegally hired U.S. ships to capture British ships. He also made plans to capture Louisiana by attacking the important city of New Orleans. Genet's efforts angered many Americans.

21

Genet was asked to leave the country, but he never did.

Throughout the 1790s, the United States worked to keep good relations with Britain, France, and Spain. In 1794, John Jay drafted a treaty with Britain. The treaty, called Jay's Treaty, said that the United States and Great Britain would share "universal peace, and a true and sincere friendship."

Jay's Treaty worried the Spanish. They felt that America and Great Britain might now work together to attack Spanish Louisiana. In 1795, Spain tried to win America's friendship by agreeing to let American farmers use the Mississippi River without paying a fee. The two nations signed the treaty, which was called Pinckney's Treaty. It was named for Thomas Pinckney, the U.S. **diplomat** who helped write it.

The French did not like these two treaties. Jay's Treaty gave France's enemy, Britain, a new **ally**. Pinckney's Treaty strengthened Spain's control of Louisiana. The French were already fighting Britain and several other

Thomas Pinckney was a special commissioner to Spain from 1795 to 1796.

John Adams was the second president of the United States.

nations. After Jay's Treaty was signed, France considered America its enemy, too.

In 1796, French warships began to stop U.S. ships on the Atlantic Ocean and seize their cargo. By the summer of 1797, France had captured more than 300 U.S. ships.

John Adams, who was now the U.S. president, wanted to avoid a war with France. He sent diplomats to France to discuss a way to end the attacks on American ships.

France was not eager to make peace. Soon, Congress ordered attacks on the French ships. The two nations fought from 1798 to 1800. They never officially declared war against each other. The fighting between them was known as a quasi war, or unofficial war, but the battles were certainly real. The U.S. Navy clashed with French ships a number of times. Because the American forces were so strong, France was not eager to turn the quasi war into a real one.

NAPOLÉON'S DREAM

While France and the United States were fighting at sea, Spain was making plans to leave Louisiana. The country was spending more money running the territory than it was earning from it. In 1796, Spain's prime minister, Manuel de Godoy, offered to sell Spanish Louisiana back to France. France thought that the price was too high, however, and would not accept the deal.

Three years later,

Manuel de Godoy

26

Napoléon Bonaparte was a brilliant, but ruthless, military leader.

General Napoléon Bonaparte seized control of France. A
brilliant military leader, Napoléon dreamed of expanding
the French empire into North America. He wanted to
begin by taking Louisiana. Napoléon was ready to end the
quasi war with the United States. Soon, he was discussing

27

Life for slaves on Santo Domingo's sugar plantations was harsh.

peace with America while, at the same time, making a deal with Spain.

On September 30, 1800, the United States signed a peace treaty with France. The next day, France and Spain secretly signed another treaty. It was called the Treaty of San Ildefonso. In this treaty, France agreed to trade a small piece of its land in Italy for all of Spanish Louisiana.

Napoléon prepared to send troops to his new lands in North America. First, however, they had to stop on the island of Santo Domingo to end an uprising of slave workers there. This Caribbean island was valuable to France as a source of sugar and coffee. Late in 1801, a fleet carrying 20,000 troops left France for Santo Domingo.

JEFFERSON'S DREAM

In 1801, Thomas Jefferson became the third president of the United States. He was already one of America's greatest leaders. He had written the Declaration of Independence, the document that made the thirteen colonies a free and independent country.

Jefferson wanted the new country to grow larger and stronger. He dreamed of expanding the United States across North America. He knew that Louisiana and the Mississippi River played a large part in his dream. The regions west of the Mississippi River were not yet explored, but Jefferson believed they were rich in resources. He wanted the vast lands west of the Mississippi for American farmers, ranchers, and settlers. Jefferson also wanted to find new rivers for trade and transportation.

Most important, Jefferson wanted to keep the new country free. He did not want European countries along its borders, fighting for land and resources.

Thomas Jefferson was the third president of the United States.

In 1784, Jefferson had written a plan for dividing the western regions into territories, which could then become states. To become territories, the regions first had to be settled. Jefferson's dream now was to settle Louisiana—which would soon join the Union as new states.

WARNING OF WAR

While George Washington was president, Jefferson had served as secretary of state. In this role, he was in charge of America's relationships with foreign countries. The new president now faced a difficult problem with France.

Napoléon's actions worried Jefferson. The president found out about France's secret treaty with Spain. He also knew that French troops were on their way to Santo Domingo—and then, most likely, to New Orleans. Now, more than ever, the United States could not afford to have a powerful, unfriendly nation controlling the Mississippi River. Americans who had already settled in the West depended on the river for their survival.

In April 1802, Jefferson sent a letter to Robert R. Livingston, the U.S. **minister** to France. "Every eye in the United States," wrote Jefferson, "is now fixed on this affair of Louisiana." Jefferson asked Livingston to issue a warning to the French. He asked Livingston to tell them that

32

the United States would join forces with Great Britain to stop Napoléon.

Livingston discussed this serious matter with Napoléon's brother Joseph and others. He told them that France would have a hard time controlling Louisiana. He also told them that the United States might want to buy New Orleans and Florida. Spain owned Florida, but Livingston thought France could convince Spain to sell it. The French did not respond to Livingston's ideas.

Robert R. Livingston

Tensions rose in October. Spain refused to allow U.S. ships to sail into New Orleans. At the same time, France took control of Louisiana. Once again, Americans talked of war— against France or Spain. President Jefferson, however, did not want a war. He still hoped he could end the crisis peacefully.

A GREAT BARGAIN

Early in 1803, President Jefferson sent James Monroe as his representative to France. The president had ordered Monroe to buy New Orleans and Florida—for almost $10 million.

The day before Monroe arrived in France, Livingston met with the French foreign minister, Charles-Maurice de Talleyrand-Périgord (more commonly known as Talleyrand). Livingston had spoken with Talleyrand before, but

Charles-Maurice de Talleyrand-Périgord

now the minister surprised him with a new offer. Talleyrand said that if the French gave away New Orleans, the rest of Louisiana would no longer have any value to them. Talleyrand asked Livingston what the United States would "give for the whole."

Toussaint-Louverture

Selling Louisiana was Napoléon's idea. His dream of a new French empire in North America had crumbled. Under the leadership of Toussaint-Louverture, the slaves on the island of Santo Domingo were defeating the French troops. Napoléon had planned to bring supplies from New

35

Orleans to the island. If he no longer controlled Santo Domingo, he no longer needed Louisiana. Napoléon was also planning to fight new battles in Europe. The sale of Louisiana would give him the money he needed for his troops.

Livingston told Monroe about Talleyrand's offer. The two Americans were not sure what to do. The president had instructed them to buy New Orleans and Florida—but the chance to buy all of Louisiana was too good a **bargain** to ignore. The offer did not include Florida, but the French hinted that the Americans could probably take the region from Spain.

Livingston and Monroe finally offered $15 million for Louisiana—about 3 cents per acre (7.5 cents per hectare). The French accepted. On April 30, 1803, the two countries drafted the treaty that made Louisiana part of the United States. This famous deal, known as the Louisiana Purchase, doubled the size of the United States and greatly increased its strength as a nation.

A Great Nation

President Jefferson was thrilled that Louisiana now belonged to the United States. American ships could now travel freely along the Mississippi River. America could begin to settle the vast lands between the Mississippi River and Pacific Ocean. Jefferson's dream was finally coming true—but not everyone was as happy about the purchase as he was.

Americans James Monroe and Robert R. Livingston complete negotiations for the Louisiana Purchase with French foreign minister Charles-Maurice de Talleyrand-Périgord.

37

Jefferson planned to offer the unsettled areas of the West to the Native Americans who were already living in the region. As white settlers moved west, he hoped the Indians would move, too, trading their native land for the new areas he had set aside. Unfortunately, President Jefferson did not foresee the years of terrible hardship that Native Americans would suffer as they were forced to leave their homelands.

People in the East were unhappy, too. They feared that their states would become less important as more Americans moved west. Some, like Senator Samuel White of Delaware, feared that Western settlers would begin to view Easterners as "strangers." They feared that the United States would no longer be "united." Others believed that Jefferson did not have the right to buy Louisiana and make it part of the country. They believed that he had gone beyond the powers given to the president by the U.S. Constitution. Despite these objections, in October 1803, Congress approved the Louisiana Purchase—six months after the sale.

This drawing by Patrick Gass, a member of the Louis and Clark Expedition, shows a council with Native Americans.

The United States now owned all the lands west of the Mississippi to the Rocky Mountains, an area of more than 800,000 square miles (2 million square kilometers). The territory also stretched into what is now Canada. The exact borders of Louisiana were not known, however. No European had ever traveled throughout all of the region.

In 1803, America began preparing to explore the newest part of the country. Before the French even offered to sell Louisiana, President Jefferson had asked Meriwether

Lewis and William Clark to explore the western regions. William Clark was the brother of George Rogers Clark, the man whom Jefferson had asked to explore the West in 1783. In May 1804, the Lewis and Clark Expedition left St. Louis on a two-year mission to find a route to the Pacific Ocean. They planned to draw maps of the region and also to develop diplomatic relations with Native Americans.

The Louisiana Purchase and the Lewis and Clark Expedition drew America's attention to the West. People now knew that the United States would soon stretch from the Atlantic Ocean to the Pacific Ocean. Settling the vast frontier of Louisiana took many years, however. The final borders were drawn in 1818 and 1819.

The Louisiana Purchase was the largest purchase of land in American history. This great parcel, called the Louisiana Territory, formed all or part of fifteen states. They are Louisiana, Missouri, Arkansas, Iowa, North Dakota, South Dakota, Nebraska, Oklahoma, Minnesota, Montana, Wyoming, Colorado, Kansas, New Mexico, and Texas.

Within 100 years after the Louisiana Purchase, the country had been settled from the Atlantic Ocean to the Pacific. As Livingston had said, when the United States made the Louisiana Purchase, the young nation took its place "among the powers of the first rank."

A tent city in Oklahoma just after the land was opened to settlers in 1889

41

GLOSSARY

ally—a friend or helper

bargain—a good deal; something that costs less than the usual price

diplomat—a person who manages a country's affairs with other nations

expedition—a long journey made for a special purpose

minister—a person who represents a government in a foreign country

purchase—(noun); something that has been bought

rebels—people who fight against a government or ruler

rival—a person, or country, competing with another for the same goal

territory—a large area of land

treaty—an agreement between two governments

DID YOU KNOW?

- Lewis and Clark asked an Indian woman named Sacagawea to travel with them as their guide. Her image appears on the golden dollar that was issued by the United States in 2000.

- Before he became president, Thomas Jefferson wrote the Declaration of Independence and the Virginia law that protected freedom of religion.

- In 1812, Louisiana was the first state admitted to the Union from the Louisiana Purchase.

- In 1912, New Mexico became the last state to be created from the Louisiana Purchase.

IMPORTANT DATES

Timeline

1682	France claims land in North America and names it Louisiana.
1718	The French establish the city of New Orleans at the mouth of the Mississippi River.
1783	The Treaty of Paris is signed; eastern Louisiana becomes part of the United States.
1798	The United States and France begin a two-year quasi war.
1799	Napoléon Bonaparte takes control of France.
1800	Spain secretly agrees to give Louisiana back to France.
1802	France takes control of Louisiana; Toussaint-Louverture leads a slave rebellion against the French on the island of Santo Domingo.
1803	France sells Louisiana to the United States.
1804	Lewis and Clark begin their expedition to explore America's new frontier.

IMPORTANT PEOPLE

NAPOLÉON BONAPARTE
(1769–1821), *military genius; general and emperor of France*

THOMAS JEFFERSON
(1743–1826), *the first U.S. secretary of state and the third president of the United States of America (1801–1809)*

ROBERT R. LIVINGSTON
(1746–1813), *U.S. minister to France who helped arrange the Louisiana Purchase*

TOUSSAINT-LOUVERTURE
(c. 1743–1803), *black revolutionary leader who led a slave rebellion on the French island of Santo Domingo*

JAMES MONROE
(1758–1831), *special representative sent to France by President Jefferson to buy New Orleans and Florida; fifth president of the United States*

CHARLES-MAURICE DE TALLEYRAND-PÉRIGORD
(1754–1838), *French foreign minister who helped Napoléon sell Louisiana to the United States*

WANT TO KNOW MORE?

At the Library

Blumberg, Rhoda. *What's the Deal? Jefferson, Napoleon, and the Louisiana Purchase*. Washington, D.C.: National Geographic Society, 1998.

Gaines, Ann. *The Louisiana Purchase in American History*. Berkeley Heights, N.J.: Enslow Publishers, 2000.

Herb, Angela M. *Beyond the Mississippi: Early Westward Expansion of the United States*. New York: Lodestar Books, 1996.

Kozar, Richard. *Lewis and Clark*. Philadelphia: Chelsea House, 1999.

On the Web

The Avalon Project: The Louisiana Purchase

http://www.yale.edu/lawweb/avalon/amerdipl.htm

To read important original documents, including the Treaty of San Ildefonso, the Jay Treaty, and the Louisiana Purchase Treaty

New Perspectives on the West

http://www.pbs.org/weta/thewest/program/episodes/

A companion web site to an eight-part television series on America's West. "Episode One" presents information about the region through 1806— including the stories of the native peoples, the European explorers, the American settlers, and the Lewis and Clark Expedition.

Through the Mail

The Louisiana State Museum

The Cabildo

701 Chartres Street

New Orleans, LA 70116

For information on the early history of New Orleans and the Louisiana
Purchase

On the Road

Jefferson National Expansion Memorial

11 North Fourth Street

St. Louis, MO 63102

314/655-1700

To visit the Museum of Westward Expansion and ride to the top of the
Gateway Arch, the 630-foot (192-meter) memorial that honors the Lewis
and Clark Expedition

47

INDEX

About the Author

Michael Burgan is a freelance writer of books for children and adults. A history graduate of the University of Connecticut, he has written more than thirty fiction and nonfiction children's books for various publishers. For adult audiences, he has written news articles, essays, and plays. Michael Burgan is a recipient of an Edpress Award and belongs to the Society of Children's Book Writers and Illustrators.